Preface

In today's times if you turn on the television, or read the paper it doesn't take long to realize that emergencies and disasters are everywhere. On the television we are getting reports of foreign nations at war and natural disasters everywhere. Most governments will not have the capability to take care of you and your family in such circumstances. Are you prepared to take care of your family for a few days to a few months?

This is the first book of a series. This book is a quick reference of goods to have on-hand during emergencies and disasters. It is not just a right but should be a responsibility for everyone to be able to take care of their families and hopefully get their communities to be prepared as well. Let's face it, if total chaos breaks out, governments have their safe havens to go to but we normal citizens can't afford to build underground bunkers that can take care of 100 people for 5 years.

The secret to survival is to be able to continue a semi normal environment. One should strive to eat most of the same foods, drink the same drinks and be able to somewhat control a comfortable environment. The key to becoming a prepper is persistence. I know that we all don't have 10's of thousands to invest on goods but if you go to the store to buy a bag of beans, don't just buy one bag but buy two and put one back.

Personally, I started back with the Y2K crisis, getting myself prepared. As I knew what the possibilities could be if the computers went down. I didn't have an $80,000 a year job but had a meager pest control technician wage. It took me many years to get somewhat supplied on what I thought I needed for me and my family to survive. The quicker you get started the quicker you reach your goal on what you will need for your family and location. Now let's get started.

Get the following documents together. We suggest a waterproof container, as simple as a Ziploc bag. Start with the easiest, drawing a line through items as you complete them. Do what you can, as quick as you can; finish as time allows.

LEGAL/IMPORTANT DOCUMENTS
- ➤ Identifications:
- Driver's License or State I.D.
- Passports
- Social Security Cards
- Birth Certificates
- Family photos showing everyone together

➢ Other Licenses/Certifications/Degrees: Military, LEO, Medical, Firearms, etc.

➢ Financial Information: (and include specific contact Information – *see your statements*)
▪ Bank Accounts (including Safety Deposit Box Information)

▪ Debit Card Numbers

▪ Credit Card Numbers

▪ Contact Information for Any Benefits You May be Receiving - Social Security, SSI, Retirement, Annuities, etc.
➢ Housing Information:
▪ Mortgage/Deed to House

▪ Rental Agreement(s)

▪ Closing Documents from Title Company

▪ Property Tax Statement (if applicable)

▪ Utility statements & Contact Info for Each
➢ Wills

➢ Power(s) of Attorney (for you and/or elderly parents)

➢ Directive(s) to Physicians

➢ Important Contacts: Phone/email list, including out-of-state numbers – not everyone…just 5-20 *important* contacts

Emergency Survival Made Easy 615-568-0051 Smyrna, TN 37167 www.EmergencySurvivalMadeEasy.com

- ➢ Medical Information:
- ▪ Prescriptions *(don't forget eye glasses & contacts)*

- ▪ Physicians' Names & Contact Numbers

- ▪ Copies of Medical Records

- ▪ Allergy List

- ▪ List of Special Conditions – e.g., Diabetic, Heart Meds, Asthma, Seizures
- ➢ Insurances:
- ▪ Homeowners' and/or Renters'

- ▪ Medical Coverage

- ▪ Life Insurance – Term, Regular, AD&D, Long-Term
- ➢ Vehicle Information (on Cars, Trucks, Boats):
- ▪ Title(s)

- ▪ Registration

- ▪ Proof of Insurance

FOR CHILDREN AND/OR PETS

- ➢ Children's fingerprint cards – check with your local police departments; most will do this for you without keeping a copy

- ➢ Children's school registration or school contact information

- ➢ Pet registration, vaccination records, veterinarian contact information

Emergency Survival Made Easy 615-568-0051 Smyrna, TN 37167
www.EmergencySurvivalMadeEasy.com

GUIDELINES FOR EMERGENCY/SURVIVAL FOODS & STORAGE

KISS is an old anagram and truism that stands for *Keep It Simple Stupid*. This is especially important when setting up an emergency/ survival food kit.

As a general rule, a healthy adult needs approximately 2,000 calories a day to maintain normal activity.

For emergency food stores, think of what keeps on the shelf. Store dried beans and nuts in vacuum-sealed bags for a protein source. Dry pasta and rice provide the needed carbohydrates.

Dried fruit and powdered vitamin drinks give needed vitamin C, and help make safe but bad-tasting water easier to drink.

Emergency Survival Made Easy 615-568-0051 Smyrna, TN 37167
www.EmergencySurvivalMadeEasy.com

A WORD ABOUT FOOD STORAGE

The food you keep must be stored so it remains dry and free of spoilage or mold. Purchase a vacuum sealer and baggies. Store all food in the vacuum-sealed bags, and then place the bags with the food in a watertight plastic bin or container. Number-5-size buckets found at hardware stores serve this purpose quite adequately. In addition, purchase silica gel packs and place them in the bucket. These will absorb moisture, and keep the bucket and its contents dry and safe. As an alternative, there are commercially prepared dried foods and storage containers that can be purchased from several on-line companies.

SURVIVAL LIST

FOOD ITEMS
- *Bottled Water*
- Jerky
- Country Ham
- Rice, Grains, Pastas
- Non-Hybrid Garden Seeds (Fruits & Vegetables)
- Salt, Pepper
- Dehydrated Fruits & Vegetables
- All packet-type of foods (seasonings, tuna, fish, MRE's, nuts, popcorn, instant coffee, tea, hot cocoa, etc.
- Live Chickens & Livestock - when and where possible
- Some Type of Vegetable Oil or Cooking Oil

COOKING ITEMS
- Fire Starters (flints, matches, lighters, fire-starter tinder)
- Kindling/Firewood
- Propane, Lighter Fluid, Charcoal
- Kerosene, Gas, Lamp Oil
- Fuel Containers
- Aluminum Foil

Emergency Survival Made Easy 615-568-0051 Smyrna, TN 37167
www.EmergencySurvivalMadeEasy.com

COOKING ITEMS (CONT'D.)

➢ Steel or Cast Iron Pots & Pans
➢ Personal Cooker
➢ Dual Fuel Camp Stove
➢ Folding Stove
➢ Sun Oven
➢ Tri-pod – for cooking over wood fires
➢ Metal Cups, Plates, Eating Utensils, Cooking Utensils, etc.
➢ Coffee Pot & Filters

ENERGY SOURCES

➢ Gas, Diesel, Wind, Hydro, or Solar Generators
➢ Rechargeable Batteries of All Sizes – be sure to get rechargeable ones that can be recharged many times and have long life.
➢ Johnny Warmers, Hot Hands, Any Propane or Kerosene Heater
➢ Crank-up Radios, Lanterns, Alarm Clocks, Flashlights
➢ Converter
➢ Battery Flashlights, Candles, Oil or Kerosene Lamps

TOOLS

- ➤ Machete
- ➤ Folding Shovel
- ➤ Axe, Sledgehammer, Hatchet, Hand Saw
- ➤ Various Hand Tools
- ➤ Scissors, Multi-Blade Knife Set – for dressing wild animals & fish
- ➤ Bolt Cutters
- ➤ Wet Stones for Knife Sharpening
- ➤ Food Saver or Handi-Vac – along with bags
- ➤ Gardening Hoe
- ➤ Binoculars, Night Vision & Heat Seekers
- ➤ Leatherman Tool

Emergency Survival Made Easy 615-568-0051 Smyrna, TN 37167 www.EmergencySurvivalMadeEasy.com

MEDICAL SUPPLIES

➢ Polysporin
➢ Anti-Diarrheal Medicine
➢ Emetic & Anti-Emetic
➢ Aspirin
➢ Aleve, Tylenol, Pepto Bismol, Advil, Motrin, Benadryl, Cough Syrup
➢ Styptic – to stop bleeding
➢ Hydrogen Peroxide, Alcohol, Hydro Cortisone, Iodine, Sunscreen
➢ Vaseline, Hand Lotion
➢ Insect Repellant
➢ Bandages, Eyewash, Splints, Feminine Pads, Gauze, Adhesive Tape
➢ Chemical Ice & Heat Pack, Needles, Strong Thread, Q-Tips, Tweezers, Hemostats
➢ Thermometer, Bite Kits, Cotton Balls, Emergency Blankets, Beta Dine Solution
➢ Ace Bandages, Sling
➢ Antibiotics, Any Necessary Prescription Drugs
➢ Vitamins, Herbs
➢ Inhalants, Burn & Pain Treatments
➢ Medical Field Surgical Kit
➢ Silver Shield *(contact Lorraine Andrews at landrews@xplornet.com)*

PERSONAL & HOUSEHOLD ITEMS

➢ Shampoo, Soap, Conditioner, Baby Wipes, Deodorant, Toothbrush, Toothpaste

➢ Razor, Razor Blades, Shaving Cream, Beard/Mustache Trimmer

➢ Corn Starch Powder

➢ Scrubber Sponges, Steel Wool

➢ Dish Soap, Laundry Soap, Bleach, Borax, Vinegar, Windex

➢ Toilet Paper & Paper Towels

➢ Solar Shower

➢ Water Containers – all sizes from canteen to water bottle to 5-gallon collapsible

➢ Water Purifier, Water Tablets

➢ Rubber or Disposable Gloves

➢ Eye Glasses Repair Kit

➢ Trash Bags

Emergency Survival Made Easy 615-568-0051 Smyrna, TN 37167
www.EmergencySurvivalMadeEasy.com

DIRECTIONAL EQUIPMENT
➢ Compass – military style as well as digital, and a drawing compass
➢ Topography Map of Your State
➢ Various Maps for Local, State, Country

RADIOS
➢ Short-Wave Radio
➢ GMRS or FRS Frequency 2-Way Radio
➢ CB's, Ham Radio
➢ Two Police Scanners of Different Types
➢ Weather/Public Alert Radio

MISCELLANEOUS

- ➤ Housing:
- ▪ Tents & Tent Stakes
- ▪ Tarps
- ▪ Sleeping Bags
- ▪ Hammocks
- ▪ Self-Inflating Sleeping Mats
- ➤ Blankets - Regular & Solar
- ➤ Backpacks
- ➤ Rolls of Plastic, Glue, Super Glue, Duct Tape, Rope, Bungee Cord, Twine, Clear Tape
- ➤ Yo-Yo Fishing Reels, Fishing Poles, Fishing Reel Oil, Line, Hooks, Sinkers, Bobbers
- ➤ Live & Regular Traps
- ➤ Siphon Tube, Portable Toilet, Hand Can Opener, Rain Barrel w/Lids
- ➤ Coolers, Portable 12v Coolers
- ➤ Pens, Paper, Pencils, Digital Tape Recorder
- ➤ Bikes, Bike Pumps, Towable Carts, Tire Patches
- ➤ Reading & Sun Glasses
- ➤ Playing Cards, Recipe Books
- ➤ Chains or Snatch'Em Straps
- ➤ Gas Mask, Personal BioChemical Suit

Emergency Survival Made Easy 615-568-0051 Smyrna, TN 37167
www.EmergencySurvivalMadeEasy.com

MISCELLANEOUS (CONT'D.)

- Fire Extinguishers
- Whistles & Mirrored Signaling Devices
- Self-Protection Device(s)
- Sea Foam
- Flotation Device – preferably a portable boat w/motor

CLOTHING

- *Lots* of socks
- Gloves, Hats, Good Sneakers
- Two Pairs of Boots
- Insulated Coveralls or Snowmobile Suit
- A Good Mix of Light & Dark Color Clothes
- Insulated Long Johns, etc.

**NOTE: When it comes to boots, socks, hats, winter gloves, sleeping bags, tents, and insulated coveralls/snowmobile suits – make sure that you get the best quality possible. *DO NOT GO CHEAP ON THESE ITEMS!!*

PET OWNERS

If you plan to bring your cat(s) and/or dog(s), remember their needs:

- Food
- Water Container
- Leashes, Harnesses, Collars w/Current Tags
- Tie-Out Line w/Ground Stake and/or Pet Carrier or Containment Device
- Pet Sweaters Where Applicable

* BE SAFE * BE SMART * BE PREPARED *

SUMMARY

We will discuss strategy in another book in this series, however I would like to take this time to cover a few more things for you to consider. The first thing that you will have to do is evaluate the situation. Do you stay home or do you go to a secondary location? If you choose a secondary location then you should consider taking some of your supplies there and leaving them. No matter what your decision will be you should consider purchasing a very good topography map of your state. Delorme is the company that we recommend for the topography maps. They are very detailed, very reasonably priced, and are very easy to read. The only thing that is missing with Delorme topography maps is altitude.

The most important item in survival is water. The ideal situation is for your location to have either a river or a stream nearby. The reason is that if there is ever a nuclear weapon used the fallout will float right on downstream. If you don't have this resource then maybe you could find a well with good water. Please make sure to have your well tested from time to time just to make sure that it will be safe to drink.

Even if there is a stream or river nearby water tables can and probably will become contaminated at some point. If this happens then you need to consider how you will filter or purify your water. Depending on your decision to stay home, have a secondary location, or to be mobile will determine what your procedure will be for acquiring safe potable water. Let's examine a few of the ways to achieve good water.

If you are going to stay home, have a secondary location, or have a large group of people then Berkey Water filters have some great products. If you are mobile then Katadyn offers several options, one of our favorites is the Katadyn Vario. The Paratrooper water filter is a great option for mobility, it weighs roughly 3.2 ounces and can produce 2000 liters of potable water. Lifestraws and blue lights (ultravioliet light) could be a really nice option for packing. If you know the ratio, bleach can be added to water, you could boil it, or there are purification tablets that could work as well. They all vary in size, specifications, and price.

FOOD

Food is next. There are going to be several factors in your food. One of the most important will be your health. Do you have high blood pressure or heart trouble? If you do then you may want to stay away from the MRE's or meals ready to eat. Some are loaded with sodium and fat content and are intended for healthy people that are very active to consume. An alternative to meals ready to eat would be dehydrated foods. Try to eat somewhat the same types of foods that you ate in normal times. Please don't forget your fruits and veggies. The more well-rounded diet you have the healthier you will be.

If you have any land at all one item that is fantastic would be chickens. Not only will you have meat but you will also get eggs. The eggs can be used for cooking so you will get a double benefit. If you can, make sure that you get a rooster that can replenish what you take for dinner. Unless you have deer, turkey, fish, or a lot of wildlife in your area, chickens will be very important.

Let's look at fruits and vegetables, if possible plant some fruit trees, blackberries and blueberries. Fruit will keep you healthy and is necessary.

Now on to veggies, there are two types of seeds; the first is hybrid seeds, with hybrid seeds they only bear veggies one year and one year only so if everything erodes as we know it, you will need to look into seeds that you can reuse year after year. This seed is called heirloom seed.

In years gone by you could buy pounds of heirloom seed fairly cheap but in the past few year's heirloom seed is very expensive. Get as much heirloom seed as you can.

Remember, foods that you can add to water or long term storage items are foods that will serve you and your family well. For example rice, beans, grains, and pastas all have a long term shelf life. Items like instant coffee, oats, tuna, nuts, hot chocolate, water enhancers, and popcorn will also be great items for your survival food bank.

COOKING ITEMS AND FUELS

Camp stoves, propane grills, stoves, and ovens are all used for cooking. One important issue to point out here is the fact that if it is a severe situation, you can't store enough fossil fuels to last forever, so plan ahead and look into solar ovens, wood stoves or pit cooking. Always use the fossil fuels first as eventually they will go bad. Have a good flint, a lot of matches or plenty of lighter fluid.

 If you don't have any of these readily available think about dehydration, or putting meat in salt like the pioneers did in the old days for preservation.

Some forms of energy will be invaluable. These include wind, hydro, and solar generators. Solar power will be the one used by most individuals. Keep in mind if you are going to use solar battery packs, purchase tons of rechargeable batteries. All batteries are not the same so make sure you know how many times you can recharge the battery and how many mah's they are rated for. In other words how much energy they can store. The larger the mah's the better. Crankable devices will be a plus as well, such as crank up lanterns, flashlights, and radios. Some of these devices will also recharge cell phones.

Wood will be in high demand as well. Not only will it be used for heat but it will also be used for cooking and light as well. Try to be located someplace where there are a lot of trees. I want to throw in at this point that depending on the circumstances we will be going back to the pioneer days where families lived next to waterways with a lot of trees and wildlife.

TOOLS

Just like cooking items and fuels, your gasoline operated tools will be used as long as the gas holds out then they will be useless. Even if you do have a buried tank on your property, I am not for sure you want to use the gasoline powered tools. They will make too much noise and everyone will know your position.

Hand tools will be very valuable. If you are fortunate enough to have a solar generator you will still be able to run some of your electrical appliances and tools. Again I can't warn enough, do NOT make noise to where everyone knows where you are at. If they know you have something they may want to take it from you.

I would recommend that you have these very important items: shovel, machete, a really good bow saw so that you can cut down trees, and a good foot operated hydraulic wood splitter. You may want to get a multi knife blade set so that you can fillet fish and process wild game. Get a good whetstone so that you can keep your cutting instruments sharp.

A good metal detector could come in very handy. I have a feeling that if a total chaotic situation broke loose that there will be a lot of usable goods buried. A hoe for gardening and maybe an old sickle to cut your grass with will be very important items as well.

PERSONAL ITEMS

This is another area that is going to be very hard to stock up on. When you get thinking about toilet paper, soaps, shampoos, cleaning supplies, and personal hygiene there is no way that you can have enough if the disaster lasts for months or years. The only recommendation that I can give you on this area is try to stock up the best that you can.

If the water in the house is not running then you will have to worry about trash and sanitation. If you have to use the restroom outdoors or have trash you will want to make sure that you are not contaminating any nearby water supplies that you are getting your potable water from.

A couple of great items that I can recommend to you will be a couple of solar showers, and reading or sun glass repair kits. With the solar shower you will be able to take a hot shower or use the hot water for a cup of instant soup or instant coffee. I would get quite a few glass repair kits, if you needed glasses to see with it will be very important to have these kits.

RADIOS

Radios will be very important but again I will warn you that the only thing that radios should be used for will be listening. The ONLY time you should talk on two way radios is for very dire emergencies. I have a short wave radio just in case that total chaos breaks out, that another country will report it just in case media doesn't cover it here. Two way radios such as walkie talkies, cb's or ham radios would be a good thing to have. Ham radios will be extremely good as they have long range capabilities.

On the police radios I have two types. The one is for the lower frequencies and the other will carry more frequencies with more channels. Technology has developed digital frequencies now that some police stations are using. The cost is still quite expensive so not very many departments and agencies will use the digital channels.

Last but not least is a good Weather/public alert radio. If you purchase one of these radios try to get one that has the SAME technology or in other words radios that can be set to only receive your county or area.

MISCELLANEOUS ITEMS

I have changed the location of this item from personal items to miscellaneous items. The item is night vision. If looting and ill will deeds take place it will usually be under the guise of night time. With night vision you will be able to see trouble heading your way before it ever reaches you. Just make sure that you have plenty of rechargeable batteries for your night vision.

If you plan on being mobile either purchase a tent or hammock. Both are really good but the only drawback with a hammock is the fact that there has to be trees so that you can have a home. I personally like tents but that is just my opinion.

Have many tarps, as you will be using them to keep firewood dry, wind breaks for tents or hammocks, or any other use that you can think of. Again if you are mobile you will want yo-yo fishing reels and snag wires. You will want to eat and hopefully you are in an area where fish and game is abundant.

A bicycle is a good alternative mode of transportation. Another good mode of transportation will be a horse but not everyone can keep a horse. Have some types of entertainment, rather it is playing cards, mp3 player or any kind of music player etc. When you are not doing chores you will need some kind of entertainment to keep your mind off the situation. Have many types of fasteners like ropes, twine, duct tape, and or bungi chords.

CLOTHES

Hopefully you have a really good mix of clothes. Multifunctional would be good but not necessary. About the most important thing I can recommend to you is that you have boots rather than shoes. Boots offers you more protection for your feet and are more rugged than shoes. Your climate in your area will dictate what kinds of clothes you should have.

Another good thing will be to have a lot of socks. You will need a lot of socks for not only the summer but also winter socks as well. Protect your feet because you will be on them for long periods of time and you will not need any foot problems.

MEDICINES

One very important medicine that I would highly recommend to you is antidiarrheal medicine. Water and food will eventually go bad and you will not need to have bad food and get diarrhea on top of everything else. Another good idea if you are on a prescription medicine you may want to find a way to get a supply held back.

Again medicines are an item that you will want to get as big of supply as possible. Remember, Wal-Mart probably will not be open or it will be getting looted in a chaotic situation. The prescriptions will be the big problem for example insulin for diabetics, blood thinners, high blood pressure pills, and hormones.

CLOSING REMARKS

As you can see it will be very hard for any one family to have everything that they will need for a long term emergency or disaster. The best thing that you can do is find a prepper group in your area or find like minded people and band together. I hope this book will get you started on your way to being able to provide for your family.

The next book that will come out in this series will be titled **"WTF America"**. In this book we will take a look at the emergencies and disasters that could possibly take place in the near future and what the ramifications could mean for you and your family.

We are Emergency Survival Made Easy.com and we invite you to visit us at www.emergencysurvivalmadeeasy.com . Here you will find other services that our company offers. Every family and situation is different and we can either provide phone consultation or the ultimate is an on-site consultation where we can provide a complete action plan for you and your family. We hope to see you again in the near future.

*BE SAFE*BE SMART*BE PREPARED*

www.ingramcontent.com/pod-product-compliance
Lightning Source LLC
Chambersburg PA
CBHW060352290526
45791CB00004B/1651